Comfort Ye My People

Revised Edition

Lionel Foster, Sr.

Copyright © 2009, 2018 Lionel Foster, Sr.

All rights reserved. No part of this publication may be reproduced, distributed, or transmitted in any form or by any means, including photocopying, recording, or other electronic or mechanical methods, without the prior written permission of the publisher, except in the case of brief quotations embodied in critical reviews and certain other noncommercial uses permitted by copyright law. For permission requests, write to the publisher, addressed "Attention: Permissions Coordinator," at the address below.

Zeta Publishing, Inc
P.O. Box 953
Silver Springs, FL 34489
www.zetapublishing.com

The views expressed in this work are solely those of the author and do not necessarily reflect the views of the publisher, and the publisher hereby disclaims any responsibility for them.

Ordering Information:
Quantity sales. Special discounts are available on quantity purchases by corporations, associations, and others. For details, contact the publisher at the address above.
Orders by U.S. trade bookstores and wholesalers. Please contact Zeta Publishing: Tel: (352) 694-2553; Fax: (352) 694-1791 or visit www.zetapublishing.com

First published by Xlibris

Rev. Date: August 2018

ISBN: 978-1-947191-62-4 (sc)
ISBN: 978-1-947191-63-1 (e)

Library of Congress: 2018930866
Printed in the United States of America

Contents

I.	Dedication	1
II.	Acknowledgments	2
III.	From The Author	3
IV.	True Liberty	5
V.	The Spirit-Filled Life	7
VI.	Transformation Of The Believer	9
VII.	Poetry	22
VIII.	Pearls Of Wisdom	50
IX.	Sonship Inheritance	66
X.	Confessions Of Faith	69

Comfort Ye My People

This work is dedicated to Jesus Christ, who through the years, has restored and preserved me; and has provided the grace, the anointing and the inspiration to deliver a message of faith and hope. Christ assuredly sustains his own, throughout the process of our transformation into His image and likeness.

ACKNOWLEDGMENTS

To Michael Renard Makel, a great nephew, with whom I in recent months, have spent quality time in meaningful and heart-warming conversation. (I have been greatly enriched for it my friend and confident!)

Many thanks to Brenda Foster, Clariese Ragins and Dawn Makel, who have been determined to make a difference!

To my Aunt Emily, Kevin and Teresa Moody, and also Evangelists Shiela and Khadiyah Hameen - all who have graciously stood by in crisis.

From the Author

This is my first sizable literary endeavor, and for more reasons than one, it has been more of a joy than a challenge. I have always been fascinated with the power of written words, to give "wings" to the mind of the reader, in a way that spoken words at times cannot. Another joy of this endeavor has been through being daily full of inspiration – compelled by the idea that I would see my work become a product done with craftsmanship.

This work consists of the first several writings brought to completion since the time I first set out to achieve proficiency as a Kingdom Scribe. Oddly enough, I became aware that I had been entrusted with the Ministry of the Scribe, when as yet any of my works (including the initial publication "Words of Wisdom") were but scattered ideas scribbled on papers here and there, for later organization.

My now deceased uncle, Mr. Benny Moody, of Spartanburg, South Carolina would ship books to our home in Baltimore, MD during my childhood days. What he did made a difference in my life! Though my grade school involvement with books was fun and enlightening; and it made its contribution to my early development, it was my uncle's contribution that made the real difference! The books he sent me seemed to be the perfect stimulus at that time.

I find it interesting that with every manuscript I have ever cited for publication – underlying each endeavor was the hope that my work would make a similar impression, as the books that my uncle sent to our home had on me.

May God bless the memory of Mr. Benny Moody and may he bless every individual in your life and mine who makes reading more enjoyable-especially if your experience with books is anything like mine!

"Comfort ye, Comfort ye my people, saith your God. Speak ye comfortably to Jerusalem and cry unto her that her warfare is accomplished, that her iniquity is pardoned: For she hath received of the Lord's hand double for all her sins."

ISAIAH 40:1-2

SECTION I
TRUE LIBERTY

TRUE LIBERTY

Everyone desires certain liberties; and realistically speaking, there are few free souls. I believe that true liberty begins with the heart of an individual, and by conditioning the mind it finds its complete expression, by its manifestation in every facet of one's existence.

I believe that a life of freedom can be experienced while yet in the midst of extenuating circumstances. I believe liberation to basically consist of having a heart free of greed, materialism, hatred toward others, selfishness, deceit, malice, envy and partiality. I deem all the aforementioned to be our chief vices and our worse enemies.

Let us not doubt the possibility of living free of these vices; because where there is life there is hope of attaining the kinds of spiritual transformation and renewal that God desires for mankind. That transformation, that renewed life liberates us from the grip of such vices! Where there is an all – enduring will, the way has already been made for the achievement of this kind of liberty.

After experiencing such liberty (to whatever extent), let us not be deceived with the grand delusion that being at liberty is to live pain exempt and trouble free! Quite to the contrary, liberty, with all its privileges, carries certain grave responsibilities which are unique to the realm of liberty. Among those responsibilities is the obligation of servitude – the responsibility of helping others to improve the quality of their lives – which is helping them to freedom!

After answering the question of and accepting the challenge of "the price of freedom," one is inevitably thrust into a lifelong pursuit of freedom's realization. Desires accomplished lead to equal or greater desires to be accomplished!

Howbeit, the Word of God holds true that "where the Spirit of the Lord is there is liberty", and, "If the Son shall make you free you shall be free indeed – Jesus the Son of God, that is!

SECTION II
THE SPIRIT-FILLED LIFE

THE SPIRIT-FILLED LIFE

- Being filled with God's Spirit will spark the desire for His knowledge, wisdom and understanding; which helps to develop a good relationship with Christ.
- A good relationship with Christ and constant obedience to His word affords: spiritual life and power; mental and physical-health, strength, and overall well-being.
- The aforementioned enables us to consistently practice righteousness unto spiritual maturity.
- Practicing righteousness develops moral character and the fruit and gifts of God's Spirit in our lives; and gives Christ a sure basis on which to prosper us!
- All the above enable us to freely serve Christ and others!
- Diligent service to Christ and to others will kindle the desire for, and bring the wisdom and wherewithal for effective witnessing and soul-winning.
- Diligent service to Christ and to others will also bring increase to spiritual and material substance. They provide support and provision, and also enable us to help finance Kingdom endeavors.
- Together these principles and provisions will aid us in achieving our goals and ambitions, in the pursuit of our God-given purposes.

SECTION III
Transformation Of The Believer

Lionel Foster, Sr.

To the soldiers of Christ (both past and present) who, upon conversion, have set out to strengthen the brethren and whose endeavors to do so have been undergirded with the transforming power of the Master Himself.

Contents

1. Transformation, The Crucial Process
2. Transformed Unto Newness of Life
3. Spiritual Development Through Transformation
4. The Soul's Prosperity Through Transformation
5. Transformation Unto Holiness
6. The End Result of the Transformation Process

INTRODUCTION

The transformation of the Believer is reflective of a life revolutionized by the Holy Spirit, through suffering and experience with God – suffering which proved to be for the sake of the furtherance of the Gospel of Christ.

I believe that the truths contained in this message will deepen your perception, and broaden your understanding of the will of God, not only for your life; but His will for mankind – especially the Christian Church.

I believe this message will also answer some questions for you about Christianity as we know it today, and as God intends for it to be, as outlined in the scriptures.

CHAPTER I

Transformation, The Crucial Process

The father God is concerned that all people experience not only the new birth by way of His Son Jesus Christ; but it is also His will that after experiencing the new birth, we move on to transformation by the renewing of our minds. Many believe that the new birth is enough – that it is the extent of God's requirement of the believer as it relates to spiritual development.

In John 3: verse 3, Christ referred to the new birth as being "born again" ("Verily I say unto you, except a man be born again he cannot see the kingdom of God.") The new birth is the simultaneous quickening (or making alive) of the spirit of an individual, and the regeneration of the soul!

This is what transpires upon acceptance into the family of God through true repentance from sin and the former lifestyle. On the other hand, being transformed by the renewing of the mind is a process! In Romans 12:1, 2 Paul exhorts, "Be not conformed to this world, but be transformed by the renewing of your mind, that you may prove what is that good, and acceptable, and perfect, will of God.

Most believers in Christ never experience the transformation God desires for His people. Generally they advance no further in the process of spiritual development than the initial stage, which is salvation, or "conversion" of the soul. This is the reason for the spiritually stagnated, carnal condition of so many believers.

Many are under the grand delusion that they have a close relationship, and/or favor with God, because they know of Him or have knowledge of His Word! Actually, anyone who has not been transformed by the renewing of the mind does not have a close relationship with Christ. (See Romans8:6-7). Those who are under this delusion may actually be firm believers. Often they are those who attend church religiously, or at least, regularly. They may give of their time, their talents, their energy and their resources to spiritual endeavors. They may consistently devote themselves to the overall function of the church, yet year after year they remain void of agape love; therefore they have a mindset of vain religion – having a form of godliness but denying its power! (See II Tim. 3:5). Without this transformation, the believer remains destitute of spiritual understanding, though he or she may possess a vast knowledge of scripture and even preach or teach the word of God, or prophesy it! Though they are sometimes very spiritually gifted individuals, they remain on the outskirts of the abundant life and the power of God's Spirit – the power to live a changed life in their family life or in society.

There are many religious leaders who fit this description; howbeit not everyone who fits the foregoing description desires to remain in that state. In many instances these individuals have experienced the new birth but are unaware of God's requirement of man regarding spiritual transformation, and that is, the growth contingent on the knowledge found in Romans 12:2.

As true disciples of Christ approach a lifestyle of righteousness, holiness and sanctification unto God, it behooves us to bear in mind what is stated in the scriptures in Philippians 2:5-6, "Let this mind be in you, which was also in Christ Jesus, who being in the form of God, did not consider it robbery to be equal with God". Therefore, the disciple of Christ can fully anticipate a mental makeover as a result of the mind's renewal through and by the Word of God, which brings about that great Transformation spoken of in Romans 12:2.

CHAPTER 2

Transformed Unto Newness Of Life

Upon the initial conversion – or salvation, God calls each believer to undergo suffering of tribulation in the form of situations and circumstances that are, in a real sense, as shameful to us, as Christ's afflictions were to Him. It is written that He "endured the cross, despising the shame". It is required of His disciples that we "go forth to Him outside the camp, bearing His reproach" (Hebrews 13:13). These afflictions are designed to crucify (with our cooperation) the deeds of the sinful flesh (that is, our bodies), because the Christian life requires daily dying to worldliness and fleshly lusts.

The afflictions God allows us to undergo are also designed to uncover and destroy the carnal mindset, attitudes and motives. The Christian is called to the diminishing of himself through death to the fleshly nature, that the person with the Holy Spirit dwelling in him or her may become more and more like Christ daily, and be displayed to the world as a light in darkness.

This, the place of crucifixion is where many believers drop out of the Christian race! Jesus said, "Whoever desires to follow me, let him deny himself, take up his cross daily and come after me".

Apostle Paul is quoted as saying, I am crucified with Christ, nevertheless I live; yet not I who lives but Christ that lives within me, for the life that I now live, I live by faith in the Son of God who loved me and gave himself for me. For those who will enjoy newness of life and abundant life beginning right here in the present world – crucifixion of the old life (that is, the fleshly lifestyle) is an inescapable reality! The good news is that, even in the midst of dying to self, we have the assurance of God's comfort through and by the Holy Spirit. (II Corinthians 1:3-10) We can undergo the necessary trials and the tribulation willingly, knowing that God will not permit them to become unbearable! Transformation of the spirit, soul and mind takes place as a result of that daily dying, followed by the constant quickening of our spirits, by the Holy Spirit, unto new and abundant life! Through that newness of life, we become more and more like Christ daily, through suffering (I Cor.15:31). The quickening of our spirits and the total renewing of the mind leads ultimately to the believers' complete transformation into Christ's image and likeness (Gal 4:19).

We have the assurance that even the process of transformation which is at times costly and painful, works for our good, when we apply the exhortation of Romans 12:1 and 2 to our lives. As the believer experiences transformation as I just described it, and as a result is gradually raised to new and abundant spiritual life, he or she is thereby empowered to walk in the Spirit, not fulfilling the lust of the flesh.

We are also empowered thereby to walk in love and forgiveness toward others, walking in faith, righteousness and overcoming power – possessing the power to resist the devil that he may flee from us and to be steadfast, unmovable, always abounding in the work of the Lord!

CHAPTER 3

Spiritual Development Through Transformation

At the time of the new birth (or, being born again"), we receive God's Spirit for the first time, as he begins to dwell in the believer as His temple, (John 4:3)

Then, there must be the fundamental development of the spirit man, as God by His Spirit renews the spirit of the mind. As we grow to spiritual maturity we begin to experience greater obedience to the word of God. As a result we experience greater joy in our lives. Before we can experience fullness of obedience and fullness of joy in Christ, we must experience the development of the tri-part make-up of our being.

The tri-part makeup of our being consists of spirit, soul and body. The basic development of the spirit man can be achieved through adequate prayer, by meditating in God's word, fasting with prayer, the study of God's word, but most importantly by obeying God's word. Obedience to God's word also includes tithing, and giving alms and offerings according to the proportion of God's prosperity in our lives.

After the basic development of the Spirit man has occurred, the believer can begin to be established in righteousness. With time and obedience, we can experience the soulish-realm transformation that brings forth the fruit of the Holy Spirit in our hearts and lives. (Gal 5:22-23)

As the fruit of the Spirit develops in the life of the believer, he or she is well on the way to having Christ being formed in them – his attributes – his characteristics – as they, as true disciples follow and serve Him.

CHAPTER 4

THE SOUL'S PROSPERITY THROUGH TRANSFORMATION

In many instances, before the believer's health and healing, social advancement and material prosperity are made apparent, the soul must reach a certain level of enrichment. The enrichment of the soul involves primarily, the soul's transformation process being already in motion. Verse 2 of the 3rd epistle of John states: "Beloved, I wish above all things that you may prosper and be in health even as your soul prospereth".

The soul's enrichment also involves (as I mentioned previously) the renewing of the mind. The renewing of the mind and the renewing of the inner man are part and parcel of the transformation of every believer who is taking on the image of Christ.

The transformation into the image of Christ is a tedious process which requires much of the believer. Tribulation, patience and longsuffering with joyfulness are among the requirement. Tribulation because, as the Apostle Paul stated in II Cor 4:16 "we die daily", but the inner man is renewed day by day.

The soul, prior to the believer's transformation by the renewing of the mind is like uncultivated fallow ground, even though the individual's spirit has been made alive through the new birth. The soul in its uncultivated state bares latent, undesirable traits; some of which surface only when we experience unfamiliar situations.

The new stimulus may include experiences such as moving into new surroundings; a new work environment; when one geographically relocates or becomes involved in public ministry; a public office, or a new relationship; (especially a marital relationship).

Situations such as the aforementioned require major personal adjustments, not only because they are accompanied by an unfamiliar set of obligations; but they may also be accompanied by more intense tests of patience and endurance than what we have ever experienced!

As we give ourselves time to adapt to new situations, we find that we are also challenged with more intense tests of our ability to walk in the Spirit, and to walk in agape love; because these areas are, for the Word's sake, proving grounds of the Christian life.

Another factor to consider regarding the soul's prosperity through transformation: David in Psalms 19:12 cries out to God: "cleanse me from secret faults." We all have secret faults! They are those traits which arise in difficult and/or unfamiliar situations. These secret faults surface especially as one develops a close relationship with Christ!

As dormant, undesirable traits surface in the face of changing circumstances, God permits "fiery trial" sufferings to act as refining and purifying agents in his furnace of affliction. (Isaiah 48:10) At times this chastisement from the Father's hands may seem grievous, and even brutal. We undergo chastisement as we submit ourselves to him. As we humble ourselves in obedience to his spirit and his word, it is in order to obtain the desired results of the test. (See Heb. 2:11).

It is a fact that God works the totality of our experience and our suffering to the transformation of our lives into something beautiful for his will, his purpose and his service, beginning with the prosperity of the soul.

In the process of the believer's transformation into the image and likeness of Christ, his soul prospers while he is in the midst of the sufferings and afflictions, as a part of the renewing of the mind; which also leads to the building of character. They are necessary for our lives to reflect Christ's attributes as his true witnesses – teaching those with whom we come in contact!

CHAPTER 5

Transformation Unto Holiness

It is a fact that they who follow Christ diligently are eventually transformed unto a state of holiness. Holiness is, in essence, the state of total consecration unto God. This takes place through sanctification by Christ Jesus (I Thess. 5:23). Hebrews 12:14 tells us that "without holiness, no man shall see the Lord". The process of holiness begins with sanctification of spirit, soul and body, by the Spirit of God, the word of God and by faith in the shed blood of Jesus Christ!

The scriptures therefore define for us the Spirit's ultimate aim for indwelling the believer; that is, to transform him or her into the image and likeness of Jesus Christ through holy living. The scriptures make mention of certain attributes God expects the believer to take on, as it relates to a lifestyle of holiness. Some of the attributes are:

- Wholeness: I Thessalonians 5:23
- Blamelessness: II Peter 3:14
- Faultlessness: Jude 24
- Perfection: Colossians 3:14

With daily repentance and in due process of time; with patient continuance in well doing, these attributes are developed in the life of the believer as primary elements of the transformation process. Holiness Unto The Lord!

CHAPTER 6

THE END RESULT OF THE TRANSFORMATION PROCESS

When the refining process runs its course, it yields glorious results. It places us in the position of total dependency upon God, His Spirit and His Word. As we undergo this process we become spiritually mature and more knowledgeable of God's nature by way of first hand experience. It makes us vessels of honor fit for the Masters' use. It is then that we are capable of responding to every challenge with confidence! The refining process that God works in the life of the believer also brings us to a place of victory and prosperity in all that we do. (Psalms 1:3)

(Back to the Original Design)

The ultimate and most glorious outcome of the transformation process in the life of the believer, takes place when we – the Body of Christ become manifest the Sons of God on this earth, by serving Him in full glory and power – reflecting His attributes – ultimately arriving at a complete transformation into Christ's image and likeness – being made a church without spot or blemish or any such thing. (Eph 5:27); that is, by Christ being formed in us perfectly, and that we grow up in Him one new man in the stature of the fullness of Christ prepared to live and reign with him forever!!!

SECTION IV

POETRY

Contents

The Hand of God

The Love of God

The Light Has Come

He So Loved Me

Coming Back To You

All Your Need

God's Word, A Prayer, A Song

The Unknown God

First Love

Solitude

Unspoken Fears

Pain and Hope

Spirit of God

His Song

Hope Deferred

We Have Overcome

Righteousness

Lionel Foster, Sr.

To Yourself Be True

Restore the Years

Creativity

Worldly Treasures

Doers Of The Word

In Your Footsteps

Won't Be As Long

Our Hope

The Hand of God

The hand of God – it holds the world,
from the strongest man to the baby girl.
and when you are troubled
And you don't know what to do,
Remember the hand of God holds you.
The hand of God – it moves on time
when there are answers we cannot find.
And when you are burdened
and don't know what to do,
Remember the hand of God holds you.

The Love of God

"I don't know why God loves me so",
(I've often heard it said).
. . . "But even though I've been untrue
He always shows he cares."
Love extends to the helpless a mighty hand;
For it constrained Christ to become a man –
To hurt and bleed just as we do.
That same love heals the deepest wounds.
Love gives and gives with no demands of gain.
It cheers all sorrows and eases all pain.
We can know in actuality why He loves us so;
For "we're flesh of His flesh, and bone of His bones".
His investment in us merits His Love you see.
And in all things He loves us unconditionally.

The Light Has Come

The days were cold and dark:
It seemed the clouds would always stay.
The light has come into my life.
I thought the pain wouldn't cease,
and it would make me pray and pray.
The light has come into my life.
Now that I can see, the hosts of hell can't turn me around.
The light has come into my life.
I've left the world behind, and now
I am gaining higher ground.
The light has come into my life.
It doesn't matter, come what may,
It will never be as dark as the past.
It doesn't matter, I'm here to stay –
I'm on my way to glory at last.

He So Loved Me

For years I gave him defiance and contempt – causing Him grief.
In return he gave me forgiveness and comfort. Even so, I gave Him
little time and attention. In return he took the time to lead, protect
and provide.
He never gave up on me, because he so loved me.
I gave Him a shattered meaningless life.
He gave me a new and exciting one.
I pledged to Him my allegiance
He promised me the earth for inheritance.
Finally, I realized that what I offered up,
was merely what was due;
for he created all things.
I could but give love and devotion –
And He alone made it possible,
Because He so loved me.

Coming Back To You

When it seems I don't know what to do,
I can rest my case by seeking you.
When my soul just can't find sweet release,
and life's tribulations steal my peace.
When there are things I don't understand,
I can come to you in prayer again.
I know I'll see you move your hand
by coming back to you again.
When life demands your saving grace,
I delight to turn and seek your face.
I know you'll move your powerful hand
when I come back to you in prayer again.

All Your Need

The Father took His time
creating the worlds –
Fulfilling the blue print
of his heart and mind.
How much more will he labor to
perfect us; the prized possession
of His design?
But just as we marvel that the
mighty Redwood began as a
tiny little seed, we must let God's
patience run it's course in us,
For God will supply all our need.

God's Word, A Prayer, A Song

"Always seemed that everyone else was stronger, smarter, more influential than we. All we had was fortitude, God's Word, a prayer and a song to begin pursuing our dream! But they say, you can't keep a good man down . . . In God's economy, chances go around . . . So we're gonna rise above to where we always belonged, even though we begin again, with just God's word, a prayer and a song.

The Unknown God

The grand misconception of God
Is that of a stern, gray old man,
Who holds a rod of cruel punishment
in his hand-whose primary objective is
to "impose" His will upon man;
(thus "robbing him of life's pleasures.")
By retaining this misconception,
one remains so very blind; for in reality God is a friend,
compassionate and kind,
who grants for mere happiness
A spirit of everlasting joy and gives ear to and answers
all the prayers we voice.
Who says serving God isn't fun?
There are several joys for each forsaken pleasure – yes,
each and every one!

First Love

Got down on my knees one night to pray,
Not knowing exactly what it was I'd say;
But as I thought of the struggles of that day,
the words soon followed and I voiced my concerns.
I hadn't given it much thought till then;
But I knew in my heart I yearned deep within
to return to my first love.
Why are we the last to realize we've drifted away?
It all begins when along the path we exchange God's
sweet love for pleasure.
It begins when, with worldly things we toy –
Unaware that that's the reason for the monstrous void,
and the painful, devastating mess.
After a while we come to realize we've lost the Father's address.
In case you haven't given it much thought till now,
Your heart may be seeking that blessed "somehow"
to return to its' first love.

"Solitude"

The Holy Spirit's at His best
when you're experiencing the test of solitude.
Yes, God will have his way
when for seasons you're forced to stay in solitude.
Paul's witness while in confinement
was greatly reinforced.
His limitations became opportunities
(revelation onto paper he endorsed.)
It's only for a while,
a very temporary trial is solitude.
The Holy Spirit's at His best
when you're experiencing the test of solitude.

Unspoken Fears

The world is full of lonely people –
Broken-hearted sheep with many unspoken fears –
Driven at the soul, whose pain yearns to be released
with a seeming perpetual longing.
We are "sons" whose power awaits manifestation.
Daily I live with that realization –
(Vessels conceived in great and deep waters,)
whose port is determined by "The Highest",
whose awesome hand steers the bow
toward home eternal, from the time of that conception
on into a glorious forever,
celebrated with shouts of conquest
won amid the monumental struggle of many
unspoken fears.

Pain and Hope

While in insolated existence I've often said
". . . it's merely the loneliness I dread,"
When for long, long seasons I found myself,
Alone with God and no one else,
to comfort a heart that seemed to bleed,
from the wounds of a life plaqued with needs.
But I knew my life wouldn't remain that way:
with God's help I'll find an even brighter day,
Wherein my need is met to full,
In the richest blessing possible.

Spirit of God

Heavenly dove so mysterious, yet so very familiar –
Invisible, but oh so tangibly creative,
In view of your work of recreating those
in whom you dwell.
You are like the wind, yet you abide within.
God's person dwelling in us forever:
So gentle, but so awesomely powerful.
Sweet spirit, you make music in the hearts
Too deaf to hear a note,
And upon lips too stammering to sing one.
You create in life's winter a warm glowing fire within.
You pour oil upon the wounds of humanity.
You're gentle enough to soothingly massage
my aching mind and emotions,
until I am enough consoled to rest in Him once again.
Wind of God upon which my spirit soars
above life's clouds of adversity,
I rest in the assurance that you will lead me
Through this wilderness until I arrive safely home.
Lead on eternal spirit.

His Song

Your life is a song,
Played loud and strong
By the one who loves you most and knows you best:
and the melody in His.
His golden love is the theme
Of which all nature sings.
Others listen to the song and fly with
Him on spiritual wings.
His melodic voice, to which none compares,
will bear them up and take them there.
All the works of God you do, will inspire them
to good works too!
For the inspiration is hard to deny,
So they mount those spiritual wings and fly.
You are God's song –
A melodic expression of His highest praise.
His work in you is music,
To his own glory He will use it.
For you are His song.

Hope Deferred

A dream, a hope deferred,
How many times can the soul endure?
Maybe many, maybe few; for whom is
the victory ever sure? The saintly?
The rich? The social elite, the strong?
The one who's' the wisest, or the pure?
The highest dream or hope is realized
By him who can all things endure!

Lionel Foster, Sr.

We Have Overcome

The road is long, the way is rough
But Jesus gives us grace enough.
And when we've gone as far as we can go
The rest is up to him, we know.
We have overcome!
The time we take to lift His name,
Is effort never spent in vain.
And when we've done as much as we can do,
He'll never fail to see us through.
we have overcome!
The hard trials should never bring us down;
For our foundation's much more than sound.
Along the way, it may seem that we've lost,
but he purchased our victory when he
died on the cross.
There's no need to worry – there's no need to fear.
He's already proven that he's always near.
We have overcome through Jesus Christ our Lord.

Righteousness

Would you cherish your heart's desire if it freely came to you?
Or is that one of those noble things we all suppose we'd do?
Such as using wisely our time and money?
Achieving this brings an abundance of milk and honey!
These things we will achieve, but first, the spiritual treasures:
and not by giving priority to temporal, earthly pleasures.
There is one who cries aloud in the darkness of our nights:
"There's a wrong way and there's a way that's right!"
And not merely the way most choose to live;
but to receive the best, ones best he must give.
Could truth be its really well, well worth it?
Any His is the only way?

To Yourself Be True

Because we all sometimes need good advice,
may I share this advice with you?
No matter what your failures or achievements,
To yourself you must be true.
How true that we all possess innately
Unique gifts and talents, too.
But sometimes influences such as prejudice, hatred
And greed may dictate what we can or can't do.
These stumbling blocks will remain in our paths
Until top priority has been given to Christ our maker and
His Lordship and authority.
One may deceive himself so easily by
Building his life on lies: allowing something or
Someone else to determine his goals,
(viewing his life through another's eyes).
Because each individual's needs are unique
From those of anyone else's on earth,
It requires that one reliable source (Your Creator,)
To fulfill one's potential and worth.
Because we all benefit from sound advice,
I've shared this advice with you.
You owe it to God, to others and to yourself.
Remember, to yourself be true.

Restore the Years

In pleasures of youth we waste precious years away,
Not heeding advice from those who could show the way –
realizing now,
how not to repeat those mistakes.
But we know we can't turn back the hands of time,
so we move on from here and now,
Knowing God will make it good, (as His words says) some-
how.
God will restore the years, when others expect you to fail,
for the trials you experience.
Later in life we accept the truth, (if we're wise) –
Becoming anchored in the faith, realizing we need
God's power to run this race –
Looking forward to that blessed day when he'll
wipe away all tears –
And though we sometimes suffer great loss God assures us –
He will
restore the years.

Lionel Foster, Sr.

Creativity

Creativity, sweet wine of the soul, – filling me,
Running over, never ceasing full to flow –
From the depths of my spirit – sharpening my
consciousness, that many may eat of your precious fruit
and evermore be blessed.
Creativity, you're one who has done me never a
wrong, all the while you gave to me your precious
thought or song: unlike the proud who have little to offer
(who yet boast of their own good,)
Because in the central flow of His positive vein
Their beings have never stood.
Creativity, spirit of ability from Him
Who lit my prison with your beams of pure light,
When its flame in the night grew dim –
I give myself over to you and yield to you
the right of way,
Till at last you run your course in me,
Till God bears me up with Him to stay.
For I remember the dark and lonely times when your
glad songs I could not sing:
But now your wine flows freely whether darkness
or morning life brings.

Worldly Treasures

Rain in your life is sometimes blinding,
Especially when you're weary and worn.
Pain in your heart can make the strongest person
Wish he was never born.
Some love worldly treasures, of houses,
silver and gold.
But to experience Jesus' presence and glory
Brings joy that cannot be told.
Your way will be ever brighter
As you yield to Him your every care.
For He's preparing you right now
For the day you'll meet Him in the air.
Some love earthly masterpieces,
(things that each day grow old).
But the blessed face of Christ our Lord
is the ultimate treasure to behold.

Doers of the Word

Fashioned in the image of the Almighty:
Endued with fortitude of iron tempered in the furnace of affliction:
We are they who have been deeply and brokenheartedly convicted,
prior to recovery from any fall of folly.
God rewards all who haven't merely heard;
But who "sell out" to become doers of the word, and
who are unwilling to repeat yesterday's failures, but who also realize
that yesterday's failures are tomorrow's
triumphs, Because of the power and favor of "Love" Himself.
For, had we not experienced the depths of despair,
We could not know the heights of joy;
But also remembering that no "son"
Can afford for a moment, to flirt with the time-bomb
of wickedness, for it could easily cost him and others their lives:
for our relentless adversary, both lurking and scheming,
always awaits kingdom forfeiture.
God rewards all who haven't merely heard;
But who "die out" to become doers of
The word.

In Your Footsteps

Lord, as I walk in your footsteps,
There is an increasing sense of new-found identity,
Christ consciousness and self-worth, which replaces
any sense of guilt or inadequacy,
brought on by shameful past failures.
As I follow on, I escape life's storms
before they drench me:
For my drenching would spell great detriment;
for my new form is that of a lit candle.
As I walk in your footsteps,
I readily identify with your sufferings.
I therefore realize that you lived daily with Calvary:
For mine is a series of lesser Cavalries,
Each preceded by a personal Gethsemane –
both as ever present as yours.
I now greatly anticipate a complete transformation,
for I have already experienced your
new birth and baptism.
I closely identify with your death and resurrection –
Daily dying, daily taking on new life:
For you have made me to know that renewed life
always follows death.
Through that life I am renewed by the realization
of your image and Godlikeness.
I now have a revelation of life eternal,
and I can say with new meaning "For thine is the power"
because I walk in your footsteps.

Won't Be As Long

It won't be as long as it has been.
Your great dream will soon come true.
If the wait you don't despise,
You will surely realize
the things that you set out to do.
It's always harder near the end.
Don't give up, hang in there my friend,
For, it won't be nearly as long as it has been.

Our Hope

There's a better world –
a world of wonder, splendor.
A world where the famous and not so famous
And those who were once infamous
are all equal and one.
Also many who used to be poor
and a few who used to be rich:
A world where there's no heartache,
No inhumanity or misunderstanding, or hatred;
For there is no source of these things there,
Neither any causes for them.
Heaven is that better world.

SECTION V

Pearls Of Wisdom

(A Collection of affirmations relative to God, life and the human experience) (Formerly Words of Wisdom by the same author – revised and expanded).

Comfort Ye My People

Contents

"Enlightenment"

"Fruit Trees"

"God's Militia"

"You"

"4 Awakenings"

"15 Steps to Consider"

"To Those Who Have Crucified The Flesh"

"Brief Wisdom Affirmations"

"Enlightenment"

Have you ever, (and I suppose we all have; whether consciously or subconsciously,) had your train of thought interrupted out of the blue, by the memory of an experience so profound, the education of which forever changed you for the good?

"Fruit Trees"

Each servant of Christ is, symbolically speaking, a fruit tree.

God is the proprietor of the orchard.

The greatest benefit He derives of His crops is contingent upon the

individual and the collective growth of each of His trees or vines.

The fruit is that of God's Spirit, (the fruit of which humanity is nourished.)

The proceeds from God's harvest is the Glory that he ultimately receives.

"God's Militia"

The Angelic hosts are God's "Air Force".

The Saints on the earth are His foot soldiers,

Both fighting for the same cause – the Father's "will be done."

Just when the enemy thinks he has devised the ultimate weapon to obliterate God's "lions", God causes them to soar above it by transforming them into eagles!

"YOU"

Always take into consideration that you may very well be the missing link from someone's chain of success – a missing piece to the puzzle of their destiny.

"4 AWAKENINGS OF LIFE"

- Intellectual Awakening
- Moral/Ethical Awakening
- Social Awakening
- (However; the most crucial . . .) The Awakening To The Deity of Christ

15 STEPS TO CONSIDER

1. Wise choices allow us to commit our works unto God;
2. Committing our works unto God establishes our thoughts;
3. God's establishing our thoughts leads to prioritizing;
4. Prioritizing determines our plan of action;
5. Our plan of action determines the proper course of action;
6. The proper course of action determines the extent to which we acknowledge God;
7. The extent to which we acknowledge God determines how He will direct our steps;

8. God's directing our steps leads to a sure foundation;
9. A sure foundation makes for establishment;
10. Establishment will lead to accelerated growth and development;
11. Accelerated growth and development, to prosperity –
12. Prosperity to success –
13. Success to Excellence!!!
14. Excellence in one's endeavors will bring Glory to God;
15. Bringing Glory to God will inevitably lead to one's fulfillment.

TO THOSE WHO HAVE . . . .

"Crucified the flesh" (with its lusts and affections):
To control your actions, harness the emotions;
To harness the emotions, control the thoughts;
To control the thoughts discipline the mind;
To discipline the mind, renew the mind;
To renew the mind, develop the spirit;
To develop the spirit, obey God's word,
In order to obey God's word, deny yourself;
In order to deny yourself, love God with all your heart, mind, soul, and strength;
In order to love God with all your heart; mind, soul and strength,
acknowledge Him in all your ways;
To acknowledge God in all your ways, pray always without ceasing,

as you obey His word.

WISDOM AFFIRMATIONS

- A faith-building testimony is a true success story – one of gradual, but glorious conquest by struggle.
- Anything studied and/or practiced diligently enough, we eventually become intimately acquainted with or we even master.
- What are the objects of your interest?
- Both life and time are like perpetual books of blank pages whereupon every person, by whatever deeds creates the story of his choosing.
- Life is one BIG responsibility comprised of many little details!
- Behind all of our circumstances is the mind of God and the hand of God,. making all the adjustments necessary for the perfection of His people.
- Irresponsibility and negligence in spiritual matters are the most lethal kinds of irresponsibility and negligence.
- The selfish individual will remain in the vice-grip of destitution, but the liberal person will enjoy life.
- Those who trust God the most are those who are the most severely tested and tried.
- One sorrow which accompanies wisdom is persecution from those who do not share your faith, your vision and /or your convictions – especially when one's labor is in wisdom and knowledge.

- The enemy of God and man always seeks to base his lies and accusations on something factual!
- Too often, human endurance falters at the threshold of longawaited breakthrough!
- As enlightenment comes by seeking, so peace and safety come by self-denial and sacrifice.
- Being at peace with oneself requires knowing oneself. Knowing oneself requires knowing Christ.
- Say little – pray much! Promise little – do much! Take little – give much!
- People, situations and conditions are very seldom as they first appear, and one must speak less than he knows!
- Interaction, amusement and other stimuli can merely ease or soothe the trauma temporarily;
- A song, entertainment or emotionalism may stimulate the mind and soul for hours on end; but the word of God goes to the heart of the matter – to the core of the need.
- God esteems character, the condition of the heart and quality of life far above economic status, material gain or earthly pleasure.
- Of some, he makes examples to the world that it is so!
- The present sufferings are necessary, and God always has a way more perfect than we can imagine, to bring us into the realization of His promises.
- Happiness is, arriving at your promised status in and through Christ, after seasons of trial, testing and struggle; and joy is to be in the presence of the Almighty!

- Lessons in wisdom are sometimes costly and painful; they require making mistakes and learning from them.
- Faith is demonstrated in the face of adversity; Love is proven amid harshness and cruelty; Power prevails when under pressure!!!
- The more traumatic the Christian's crucifixion (in dying daily to the fleshly nature); the more glorious the present transformation of his life and inner being.
- For the Christian, satisfaction is obtained through spiritual warfare; waging spiritual warfare requires strength, power and might; and strength, power and might are obtained through the fear of God and obeying His words.
- Deliverance from any satanic bondage or stronghold requires patience and obedience to Christ. It requires committing to a stand on unpopular convictions and directions from God.
- Our obedience to God is, the vehicle of delivery to the doorstep of others, what God intended for them before the world began.
- Good counsel makes a man resourceful to his neighbor, but the wicked seeks to destroy him.
- In God's economy, where the losses are great, the gain is eternal!
- Though true love is susceptible it is never frail; for it is the most powerful force in the universe; and to love God is to love others!
- When to God our hearts say yes, our intellects protest!

- Every relationship that appears to be had in loving oneness is not. Even a brood of vipers share the same habitation!!!
- The excitement of a thing is always greater at the onset; it's waning is not necessarily indicative of a lack of enthusiasm.
- When one compares the adversary to Christ, The enemy doesn't seem so powerful!
- The evil one is not victorious over the Godly; for Christ is the power of the righteous.
- Anyone can be silenced, but intimidation is a choice!
- Security is before confidence, and confidence comes before authority!
- Sow the seeds of discipline – reap the harvest of good results!
- One who lives close to God is highly sensitized to spiritual activity, and in most maters keen discernment is crucial.
- To each man, his cross is the heaviest!
- Never apologize for obeying God – especially not to the adversaries of God.
- It is the tendency of many to be smug about good things regarding others.
- We must be who we are until God fashions us into who we are to be.
- We will prevail if we don't sabotage our blessings, or resist our own progress by forfeiting the right opportunities.

- Seek God whom you must seek, that he may inspire you to use what He placed inside of you; that you may produce what you have to produce, that you may obtain what you need; that you may go where you need to go, in order to accomplish what you must.
- An occasional debate, unlike argumentation, can be wholesome; but the latter can be difficult to avoid.
- God grant us the patience to master the ordinary, because most of us esteem and acknowledge only outstanding accomplishment!
- Strive with specific goals in mind, and never lose sight of your purpose!
- Could it be that, God sent an angel to pipe sweet sound into the human ear; thus, music was born to the earthly sphere?
- Rehearse not your fears, but rather your triumphs!
- When one labors with God, at some point between consultation and initiation, by adversaries from more than one side, he will inevitably experience confrontation!
- With God, time, diligence and persistence you will succeed!
- Pacing yourself affords you the advantage of viewing things from more than one perspective.
- Mind not the ridicule of the young and foolish – nor the scorn of an envious elder!!!
- Commitment and contentment are alike, in that they both require abiding in God's will, regardless of one's

circumstances.

- If you are unwilling to share, you will not be in the position to receive!
- The clearer your God-given vision, the stronger your constitution, and that, the enemy knows quite well. That vision is the product of the Spirit – the revealed plan of God!
- One characteristic of manhood is to stand firm on righteous convictions, regardless of the adversities of misunderstanding, criticism and popular opinion.
- The young, the poverty-stricken and the destitute often sleepwalk through life: since life is sacred and invaluable, the enemy of God and man stalks every soul!
- Responsible leadership is the kind which leads by example: though it does not encourage the faults and frailties of others, it is patient with the weak, and strengthens them by stern instruction and verbal encouragement.
- When a society excludes the knowledge of Christ from its academic and scientific institutions and processes, its "halls of higher learning" inevitably become "dividing walls of deeper yearning".
- Spontaneity has its place; however, God has a master plan for all creation: in that sense, even for human purposes, planning leads to the success of many things.
- The enemy of God and man – both lurking and scheming, always awaits Kingdom forfeiture!

- Christ beckons us that we by responding to His call may cease to slowly commit suicide (digging our own graves through rebellion). To turn God away is to both invite and welcome death!!!
- It is possible for a man to fail at most of his endeavors and yet succeed at the things which matter most!
- None of us are all that we appear to be. At some things we are excellent – in other ways we aren't really much at all!
- Just as the love of money is the root of all evil, the person who comes to love God with all his heart, mind, soul and strength, has discovered the key to every blessing in heaven and on earth!
- While confrontation is inevitable, it is possible through wisdom, discipline and patience to circumvent its adverse influences.
- One reason that the man who has the right support system is more likely to succeed, is that he is less vulnerable to human weakness – especially the weakness of yielding to temptation.
- The strong usually become a target for the feeble-minded!
- By reason of their tremendous influences and affects – words, money and power can be instruments for good, or tools of the devil; depending upon how they are used, and by whom!
- One advantage of implementing within your plans, the input of those you know, is that more than likely you

can hold them liable for their exploitation or misuse, if any; for the simple reason that they are those about whom you have inside information!

- At certain times, God's way of penetrating our darkness is by providing anew whatever it takes for us to live in the light.
- God speaks the loudest and clearest after periods of His prolonged silence.
- Every person is alike in more ways than one, but different in ways significantly more.
- By moral conscience we are at times, coerced to choose between owning the very best or becoming our best. In such an instance we choose between "ill repair or ill repute".
- He who ascends to the mountain peak on the wings of falsehood, shall plummet as well by the gravity of truth!
- When you bleed, the jealous enjoy it – and it torments a religious murderer to see himself through the eyes of God.
- The things that interrupt your peace do not necessarily have to break your spirit!
- For the simple reason that no one can stop you from working righteousness, no one can keep you from your blessings!
- Either labor, effort or input of some sort (no matter how minute) is required of every living soul, and stability and constancy are necessary in order to succeed.
- I perceive true liberty to be possessing a heart free

of malice, envy, hatred or animosity toward others. I believe liberty begins in the heart and finds its fullest expression within every aspect and facet of one's life!

- Woman has a way of impacting a man's life in ways that are quite extreme; she will be either very good for him or very bad for him – it is not likely to be a combination of the two.
- All truth is by nature, all encompassing and ever objective!
- Just as love is stronger than the grave, loving favor transcends circumstantial barriers!
- Even after God has established you, most of your plans will not succeed without the help of your own God-given backbone and / or ingenuity!
- The enemy of God himself fuels the emotionalism and passion involved in relationships, which are based on lust or selfishness or loneliness or greed. Those entangled therein are flirting with a time bomb!!!
- The love of Christ will either form a bond between a couple; or it will free the willing party to experience and enjoy true love, with all its privileges and responsibilities.
- Darkness and light cannot occupy the same space at the same time – they cannot reside in the same heart; yet it seems that even some of the most well-meaning people find themselves trapped in "love/hate" situations!
- Trials, tribulation and adversity can be agents of God to bring us close to Him, and help to make us what

He intends – serving as stepping stones toward divine destiny!
- Those who function constantly in the love and the power of God's Spirit are both celebrated in heaven and feared in hell.
- When an individual pleases God: though scandal or controversy surrounds them – eventually the truth will prevail, and that individuals' testimony will inspire many!
- When I consider the awesomeness of God, as opposed to the rivalry of enemies, I realize that though it may appear that I am outnumbered, I am never overpowered!
- What is man but an instrument? What is his life but a record of how he was used for good or for evil?
- Love is the only weapon powerful enough to slay the dragons of hatred and indifference!!!
- There is a love that your mind could never comprehend, because it's deeper than the earth from pole to pole. When you receive it and return it, it will make you rich at heart.
- The love of God, demonstrated freely enough, consistently enough, will oftentimes bring even the abominable to repentance!
- For the faithful, life becomes full of pleasant surprises!
- Hatred is the vulture – brotherhood the dove – the word of God declares to us – all men were made of one blood!
- If a child of God can endure being branded a fanatic, insane or unsaved for well doing, as well as for his or

her downfalls, he or she can possess God's peculiar treasure even in times such as these!
- To whom is the victory ever sure? – The saintly? The rich? The social elite? The strongest, wisest, or the pure? None of these things can determine to whom real conquest is ever sure; for the highest hope is realized by him who can all things endure!
- With the help of God, any barrier can be penetrated – any obstacle overcome!

SECTION VI

SONSHIP

INHERITANCE

SONSHIP INHERITANCE

It is imperative that the people of God undergo the essential and crucial awakening, to the revelation of attaining Sonship status in God, through Jesus Christ the Lord. There must be an enlightment to the meaning of the relationship and inheritance one may enjoy right here in this present life, if he or she follows Christ for the period of time God requires. That awakening involves coming to know the rights, the privileges, the benefits and the responsibilities of the inheritance from God.

The apostle John stated in I John 3:2 "Beloved, now are we the sons of God, It does not yet appear what we shall be, but we know that when He shall appear, we shall be like Him . . ." Despite that awesome revelation, many of God's people are oblivious to the reality that they have been divinely ordained to become one with God through relationship with Christ.

Jesus Himself prayed to His Father, (In John 17:21, you will read,), "that they all may be one, as you, Father are in me and I in you, that they also may be one in us, that the world may believe that you have sent me."

We initially become one with God, through Christ, when we are baptized into Him by His Spirit. Since it is truth that believers become one with Christ through and by the spirit, we should not deem ourselves too lowly or unworthy of God that the idea of His dealing with us as His very own sons and daughters seems foreign or far fetched.

Because we become one with God through Christ, this world is not our home! As citizens of Heaven, we therefore have access to the riches and powers of Heaven. The Everlasting Father, through Christ's death on the cross, His resurrection and through His possessing all power, willed to His sons and daughters His spiritual and material blessings, as recorded in His last will and testament, the Bible.

Apostle Paul in Ephesians 1:3 wrote "Blessed be the God and Father of our Lord Jesus Christ who hath blessed us with all spiritual blessings in heavenly places in Christ. Romans 8:7

states "and if children (or sons) then heirs of God and joint heirs with Christ . . ." Paul also posed the question in Romans 8:32 "he that spared not His own Son, but delivered Him up for us all, how shall he not with Him also freely give us all things?

The Word tells us that the Sonship Inheritance, however, is not without suffering. Hebrews 12:1 states "Now no chastening for the present seems to be joyous, but grievous." We learn from the scriptures, that howbeit, the joy of the blessings outweigh the pain of suffering of our daily crosses. We can be, as our forerunner Christ the Righteous who, for the joy that was set before Him, endured the cross, despising the shame. So, when we pass God's test, His best we will possess!

There is an appointed time for the believer to attain the authority through fuller earthly manifestation of the Sonship privileges and benefits. Galatians 4:1-2 states, Now I say, that the heir differeth nothing from a servant as long as he is a child, though he be lord of all, but is under governors and tutors until the appointed time of the Father.

The condition attached to these great and precious promises: "if you endure chastening, God dealeth with you as sons, for what son is he whom the Father does not chasten" The whole world awaits the manifestation of the sons of God. (Romans 8:19) Isn't it wonderful to know that we have been brought into that adoption of sons by Him who is the firstborn of many brethren? – that is, Jesus the Christ!

SECTION VII
WEEKLY CONFESSIONS OF FAITH

WEEKLY CONFESSIONS OF FAITH

SUNDAY

I do not merely enjoy relationship with God; but also intimacy – a love so strong, an understanding so deep – absolute rest and security.

MONDAY

Father, concerning all my obligations, work in me this day, and every day to perform my duties as unto you – to your glory; for I realize that as your word clearly states, without you I can do nothing!

TUESDAY

The love of God constrains me to go the extra mile for others, considering them as though I were in their position. Hence, I fulfill the second greatest commandment – love your neighbor as yourself.

WEDNESDAY

I am, through my relationship with Christ, a channel of God's love, peace and power – power to live what I know of His word – power to effectively communicate that knowledge to others, and the power to help them experience salvation, healing and deliverance through his word and by his Spirit!

THURSDAY

I am a bold witness for Christ, and I seek the opportunity to make it so – knowing that what others need most is His Love. Therefore, I sow that love, expecting that whether apparent or not, God will give the increase!

FRIDAY

> Father I need your love to survive:
> I need your power just to climb,
> the hill on which my doubts are crucified.

SATURDAY

Only what we do for Christ will matter in the end. I spend my time giving priority to Him. Though there are other things I must get done, the source of my good results, (I realize) is my faith in God's own Son.

www.ingramcontent.com/pod-product-compliance
Lightning Source LLC
Chambersburg PA
CBHW030103100526
44591CB00008B/243